Sid and the bug

Sid is in his bed.

A big bug is on the mat.

The bug hops on Sid's bed.

Sid sits up.
Sid taps the bug.

The bug runs to the bin.

Sid is fed up!

Sid and the bug

Level 2, Set 2: Story 13

Before reading

Say the sounds: g o b h e r f u l

Practise blending the sounds: Sid bug bed big mat hops Sid's sits up taps runs bin fits gap fed

High-frequency words: in a on **Tricky words:** and the is his to into
Vocabulary check: gap – a small space between objects

Story discussion: What is the bug trying to do in the cover picture? What might happen next?

Teaching points: Check that children can say the phonemes /g/ /o/ /b/ /h/ /e/ /r/ /f/ /u/ /l/, and that they can identify the grapheme that goes with each phoneme.
Check that they can read words with apostrophes and understand they indicate possession.
Check that children can identify and read the tricky words: and, the, is, his, to, into.

After reading

Comprehension:
- What is Sid doing at the start of the story?
- Who wakes Sid up?
- Where does the bug escape to?
- Why is Sid fed up at the end of the story?

Fluency: Speed-read the words again from the inside front cover.